The Extraordinary Form of the Mass Explained

by
Fr Richard Whinder

*All booklets are published thanks to the
generous support of the members of the
Catholic Truth Society*

CATHOLIC TRUTH SOCIETY
PUBLISHERS TO THE HOLY SEE

Contents

Introduction

The Motu Proprio *Summorum Pontificum* is a short document but an important one. It has some profound implications for the way in which we understand and celebrate Catholic liturgy. The text of *Summorum Pontificum* is published separately by the CTS, and deserves to be read in full. In this short booklet, which has been inspired by the appearance of the Motu Proprio, we aim to do three things. Firstly, to place *Summorum Pontificum* in its historical context and explain the motivations which produced it. Secondly, to offer a brief history of the Mass, so that those attending the Extraordinary Form can have some idea of its development over the centuries. Lastly, we offer a short commentary on the structure of the Extraordinary Form of the Mass, which may help those attending this liturgy for the first time. Obviously there are far larger and more detailed books which can be studied by those who wish, and we offer some suggestions for further reading at the end.

The Context of *Summorum Pontificum*

'Let us generously open our hearts and make room for everything that the faith itself allows'

On 7th July 2007, Pope Benedict XVI issued a document 'motu proprio', ('on his own initiative') entitled *Summorum Pontificum*. The effect of this document was to enable far wider use of the traditional liturgy of the Church, as codified by the Council of Trent and celebrated up until the reforms following the Second Vatican Council (1962 - 1965). The Pope's document has generated a wide variety of responses. On the one hand, it has been greeted with joy by some. Cardinal Castrillon Hoyos, President of the *Ecclesia Dei* Commission which has the job of applying *Summorum Pontificum*, has described the document as 'a gift from God'.[1] Others, however, as Pope Benedict himself noted in his Letter to the Bishops of the World which accompanied the Motu Proprio, have responded negatively, and even 'with harsh opposition'. It has been suggested that the Pope is turning his back on the reforms of Vatican II - though to anyone who has read the Pope's many works referring to the Council this is clearly unthinkable, and has no basis whatsoever in *Summorum Pontificum* itself, nor elsewhere. It is not a question of rejecting any good that has come out of Vatican II - rather, it is a question of preserving the heritage of the Church alongside those reforms, and in the Pope's own phrase 'making room for everything that the faith itself allows'.

'The fruit of prayer'

What was the Holy Father intending to achieve in his Motu Proprio? He himself describes it as 'the fruit of much reflection, numerous consultations and prayer'. Clearly, it was not an action lightly undertaken. By carefully reading both *Summorum Pontificum* itself and the letter accompanying it, and by referring to writing and statements of Joseph Ratzinger both before and after his Papal election, it is possible to discern the motivations which have inspired him to undertake this initiative at the present time, as we shall now attempt to show.

A 'liturgical' Pope

Firstly, we must realise that Pope Benedict XVI has an instinctive love and reverence for the sacred liturgy that goes back many years. This is not to say that he is a 'professional' liturgist - quite a different thing - but simply that he responds at a very deep personal level to the riches of the Church's worship and that it has formed him both as a believer and a theologian. He himself has said 'the inexhaustible reality of the Catholic liturgy has accompanied me through all the phases of life', and in his book of memoirs, *Milestones*[2], he testifies particularly to the effect the liturgy had on him as a child and a young man, doing much to inspire in him his priestly vocation. Growing up in the dark days of the 1930s and '40s in Germany, the future Pope observed the way in which Catholic culture - the product in no small part of Catholic liturgy - was able to offer a genuine alternative to the poisonous doctrines of Nazism, and proved resilient enough to survive the Nazi period intact. This concern for authentically Catholic culture - and the role of the liturgy in fostering that - is one to which we shall return. For now, let us add that the Pope's deep instinctive love for the liturgy has always made him sensitive to abuses in worship, and cautious about the value of sweeping changes and wholesale reforms. Certain aspects of the renewal in worship after Vatican II have been consistently applauded by him. For instance, he has often spoken about the value of having the Scripture readings proclaimed in the vernacular, and indeed *Summorum Pontificum* makes explicit provision for this possibility in the Extraordinary Form as well. However, other aspects of the changes have sometimes worried him. Speaking broadly, we can say that there were two impulses driving the liturgical reforms after Vatican II. One was concerned to return the Church's liturgy to a more pristine state, to allow the oldest traditions to shine again through centuries of accretion and decadence. Another impulse was to adapt the liturgy to the conditions of the modern world, to make worship more relevant to the contemporary believer (or indeed, non-believer). Both these concerns have their good aspects, but they can be dangerous if pushed too far. In a book he wrote as Cardinal, *The Spirit of the Liturgy*, the future Pope compared the liturgy to an ancient and beautiful fresco. Once covered with layers of whitewash, but at least preserved from harm, the fresco was now in danger of destruction from the very people who claimed to love it: the liturgical 'experts' were like insensitive restorers, who with their harsh chemicals and extravagant theories were tampering with something they had not fully understood - while at the same time exposing it to danger from 'climatic conditions', namely the secular, utilitarian ideologies of the modern world. There can be little doubt, reading his many published works, that Cardinal Ratzinger, the future Pope, had become increasingly concerned that the Catholic liturgy was in grave danger of suffering incalculable harm. Moreover, he declared that harm done to the liturgy would result in serious harm to the Church itself, and indeed, that damage had already been done. In 2001, at Fontgombault Abbey in France, Cardinal Ratzinger called together and participated in a liturgical conference at which he said the following: 'What we previously knew only in theory has become for us a practical experience: the Church stands and falls with the liturgy'. And in another place he wrote: 'I am convinced that the crisis in the Church we are experiencing today is to a large extent due to the disintegration of the liturgy'. There can be little doubt that the provisions of *Summorum Pontificum* are in large part a response to the Pope's own sensitivities about the liturgy and the threat he sees it as facing.

Healing and harmony

As one who has himself been gravely concerned by the pace and direction of liturgical change, Joseph Ratzinger has naturally been sympathetic to others who share those anxieties. This is an experience he brings to the Papacy, and another motivation behind *Summorum Pontificum*. Indeed, he himself declares its importance. In the Letter to Bishops accompanying the Motu Proprio, he writes at some length about those people who remained attached to the traditional liturgy as celebrated before Vatican II. Some of these, following Archbishop Lefebvre, rejected all or many aspects of the Council itself, and were even prepared to separate themselves from the Church for the sake of the older liturgy. There were many others, however, 'who clearly accepted the binding character of the Second Vatican Council, and were faithful to the Pope and the Bishops' but who also wished to worship according to the older forms. In 1988, Pope John Paul II issued the Motu Proprio *Ecclesia Dei*, which sought to draw the followers of Archbishop Lefebvre back into full communion, and to encourage others attached to the traditional liturgy, by making the older forms more readily available. Cardinal Ratzinger was heavily involved, both in the negotiations with Archbishop Lefebvre, and later, with providing for those who wanted to be in full communion with the Catholic Church. With this background it is not surprising that as Pope he has done everything possible to bring an end to this harmful division within the Church, and to bring about healing. In his Letter to Bishops he writes 'Looking back over the past, to the divisions which in the course of centuries have rent the Body of Christ, one continually has the impression that, at the critical moments when divisions were coming about, not enough was done by the Church's leaders to maintain or regain reconciliation and unity'. In the current situation, at least, Pope Benedict has truly opened his heart and arms to those whose attachment to the older liturgy has caused them to separate themselves from full communion, and has done his very best to bring harmony. Indeed, the provisions of *Summorum Pontificum* have been welcomed by the followers of Archbishop Lefebvre, the Society of St Pius X, but as yet they have not returned to the visible unity of the Church. It is certainly the Pope's prayer that they will still do so.

'Interior reconciliation'

While Pope Benedict's desire to heal division in the Church is undoubtedly an important factor behind *Summorum Pontificum*, it is certainly not the case that the Motu Proprio is only directed towards the Society of St Pius X and kindred groups - although some commentators may have given that impression. On the contrary, the text of the Papal documents themselves reveal a much wider intention. The Letter to Bishops, for instance, refers to 'young persons too [who] have discovered this liturgical form, felt its attraction and found in it a form of encounter with the Mystery of the Most Holy Eucharist particularly suited to them'. The Motu Proprio is not solely directed at one group, but offered to everyone. To quote Cardinal Castrillon Hoyos, cited earlier, 'The Holy Father is willing to offer to all the people this possibility... so that everybody knows this way of celebrating the Eucharist in the Catholic Church.' In the text of the Papal Letter, Pope Benedict says to the Bishops 'the positive reason which motivated my decision to issue this Motu Proprio' was the desire for 'interior reconciliation in the heart of the Church'. This does not just refer to reconciliation with the Society of St Pius X but something deeper. To understand what this is, we should look to an earlier Papal statement. Not long after his election, in an address to the Roman Curia in

December 2005, Pope Benedict drew attention to two very different ways of interpreting Vatican II and the developments which followed it. On the one hand there is the 'hermeneutic of discontinuity and rupture'. This approach effectively suggests 'a split between the pre-Conciliar Church and the post-Conciliar Church' as if they were two entirely different things. On the other hand, Pope Benedict praises what he calls a 'hermeneutic of reform and continuity', which affirms (together with all the Popes and the documents of the Magisterium) that there is a fundamental identity between the Church before Vatican II and the Church after it. As the Pope stated in his address, 'the essential constitution of the Church comes from the Lord and was given to us so that we might attain to eternal life and, starting from this perspective, be able to illuminate life in time and time itself'. In the light of this 'hermeneutic of reform and continuity' *Summorum Pontificum* can be seen in its true significance. To quote the Pope's Letter to Bishops once again: 'In the history of the liturgy there is growth and progress but no rupture. What earlier generations held as sacred remains great and sacred for us too, and it cannot be all of a sudden entirely forbidden or considered harmful'. The virtual disappearance of the old liturgy after Vatican II (despite the fact that it was never officially abrogated, a point the Pope emphasises) was a powerful tool in the hands of those promoting a 'hermeneutic of discontinuity and rupture', suggesting some fundamental change in the Church's concept of worship. By contrast, allowing the Extraordinary Form its proper place in the Church's spectrum of worship underlines the unbroken continuity of Catholic liturgy. Indeed, a greater access to the Extraordinary Form will enable us to understand more clearly what true liturgy is, particularly if, as the Pope suggests, a greater familiarity with the older use influences the way the Ordinary Form is celebrated as well: 'The two Forms of the usage of the Roman Rite can be mutually enriching... The celebration of Mass according to the Missal of Paul VI will be able to demonstrate, more powerfully than has been the case hitherto, the sacrality which attracts many people to the former usage'.

'The power of love'

This brings us to the last and perhaps most important motivation behind *Summorum Pontificum*. It must not be thought that this Motu Proprio is some arcane or academic document, concerned with the minutiae of ceremony and ritual. Rather, it is a reflection of Pope Benedict's own over-riding priority - to make Christ and his Gospel known in the world of today. He spoke of this on a trip to Brazil in May 2007, shortly before *Summorum Pontificum* was issued. He said on that occasion: 'The Church does not engage in proselytism.

Instead, she grows by 'attraction': just as Christ 'draws all to himself' by the power of his love, culminating in the sacrifice of the Cross'. The Pope is convinced that nothing is so 'attractive' in this sense as the power of the liturgy, above all the Mass, which in its essence is nothing other than the sacrifice of the Cross made present on the altars of the Church. We have spoken before of the Pope's concern for an authentically Catholic culture, and of the place of the liturgy in making this possible. For many years, as Prefect of the Congregation for the Doctrine of the Faith, Joseph Ratzinger was on the front line of what Pope John Paul II termed a conflict between 'the Gospel of life' and 'the culture of death'. Today, as Benedict XVI, he wishes the liturgy to shine forth in all its splendour, illuminating the truth of the Gospel and drawing the faithful ever closer to Christ, the source of all love. It is not a question of preferring one form of liturgy to another, but rather of throwing open the whole treasure-house of the Church's heritage to a needy and hungry world, holding back nothing which might feed and save a hungry soul. In the words of the Pope's own beautiful appeal: 'Let us generously open our hearts and make room for everything that the faith itself allows'. That is an invitation addressed to us all.

The Historical Development of the Mass

'What earlier generations held as sacred, remains sacred and great for us too.'

In *Summorum Pontificum* Pope Benedict does not only refer to the Mass. He allows clerics the use of the Breviary of 1962, and asks pastors to provide all the sacraments for the faithful 'if the good of souls would seem to require it'. Nevertheless, the Mass is the summit of the Church's liturgy, and is the service most frequently attended by Catholics, so it makes sense to concentrate on the Mass in this brief presentation. It must be obvious that what follows is in no way a thorough history of the Mass. Rather, it offers a brief sketch, which may help those discovering the Extraordinary Form to understand why it is celebrated in the way that it is.

Origins of the Mass

The first Mass was celebrated by Jesus at the Last Supper. *The Catechism of the Catholic Church* (#1323) tells us: 'At the Last Supper, on the night he was betrayed, our Saviour instituted the Eucharistic sacrifice of his Body and Blood. This he did in order to perpetuate the sacrifice of the Cross throughout all ages until he should come again...' At the time of the Last Supper, the Apostles who were present could not fully understand the mystery they were witnessing. It was only later, after they had been instructed by the Risen Lord, and particularly after they had received the Holy Spirit at Pentecost, that they could begin to comprehend the great gift which Christ had left them. From this time on, the Eucharist became part of Christian worship, as read in the Acts of the Apostles (*Ac* 2:42). From the very beginning, it was realised that this was no ordinary meal, but a sacred rite, in which the Sacrifice of Calvary was mysteriously made present. After all, the Last Supper itself was a *ritual* meal, its ceremonies carefully prescribed by centuries of Jewish law and custom. There was no question of Jesus and his friends simply meeting for a convivial dinner party. Likewise, in the early Church, a clear distinction was drawn between the Eucharist and other festive Christian gatherings. St Paul, writing to the believers in Corinth, (1 *Co* 11) rebukes them for obscuring this distinction, and carefully lays down the proper way in which the liturgy was to be celebrated.

Roughly a century later, we have the first record of Mass as it was celebrated by the Church at Rome, c.150 AD. This is given to us by St Justin, a philosopher turned theologian, in his work the *First Apology*. Justin describes many elements which will remain constant throughout the history of the Church. The Mass is celebrated on Sunday: there are readings from the Old and New Testaments, followed by a homily. After Bidding Prayers and the Kiss of Peace, bread, and wine mixed with water are brought to the celebrant who offers them in a sacrificial prayer concluding with a doxology. Communion is given, and is taken by deacons to the sick. St Justin emphasises the Real Presence of Christ in the Eucharist: 'For we do not receive them [the consecrated elements] as common bread and common drink, but as the flesh and blood of Jesus'.

St Justin lived in a persecuted Church - and himself died a martyr. It was not to be expected that ceremony and ritual would flourish under such conditions. But the records we have of candlesticks, lamps and sacred vessels confiscated from house churches by the pagan authorities show that the Christians wished to use the best they had in the service of God. They were willing and ready to add magnificence to their celebrations when the opportunity arose.

This became possible once Christianity was made legal in the 4th Century AD. Public places of worship could now be built, and were. An early description of such a church comes to us from the pen of Eusebius, one of the earliest historians of the Church. Writing in Books 8-10 of his *Ecclesiastical History*, he describes a church built shortly after Christianity was first tolerated. The donor of the church, he writes, 'when he had thus completed the temple, provided it with lofty thrones in honour of those

who preside, and in addition seats arranged in proper
order throughout the whole building, and finally placed in
the middle the holy of holies, the Altar, and that it might
be inaccessible to the multitude, enclosed it with a
wooden lattice-work, accurately wrought with artistic
carving, presenting a wonderful sight to the beholder. And
not even the pavement was neglected by him; for this too
he adorned with beautiful marble of every variety...' This
picture of the church gives us a good impression of the
solemn, dignified and increasingly elaborate way in which
the early liturgy was carried out.

While speaking about architecture, we may say a word
about the position of the altar. In celebrations of the
Extraordinary Form, it is often said that the celebrant
'turns his back' on the congregation while reciting the
prayers of the Mass. In fact, this is a misunderstanding of
a practice which goes back to the very earliest days of the
Church. As historical research has shown us, the early
Christians always preferred to face East when celebrating
the Eucharist.[3] This was because the East, the direction of
the rising sun, was believed to be the place from which
Christ would return at the Last Judgement. In many
places, therefore, the altar itself was placed at the Eastern
end of the church. The celebrant, when offering the
Eucharistic Prayer, would stand in front of the altar, facing
in the same direction as the whole of his flock and leading
them in prayer. In other places, such as Rome, the altar

was at the Western end of the church. The celebrant, in order to face East, stood behind the altar, facing down the church. It seems likely, however, that the congregation turned Eastward too for this part of the Mass - that would explain the deacon's invitation '*conversi ad Dominum*' (let us turn to the Lord) which we find placed before the Eucharistic Prayer in many of the ancient liturgies.[4] In any case, the concept of 'facing the people' for the Eucharistic Prayer is a very modern one, and can have the unfortunate effect of placing too much emphasis on the celebrant. By contrast, when priest and people are all facing in the same direction for this prayer, as is invariably the case in the Extraordinary Form (and is an entirely legitimate practice in the Ordinary Form as well[5]) the ancient image of a Church turned towards its Saviour is preserved.

The Age of St Gregory the Great

Pope Gregory I, the Great, is singled out for special praise in *Summorum Pontificum*. He holds a special place in the history of the liturgy, because most scholars believe that it was during his pontificate that the Roman Rite crystallised in all its essential elements. What were those elements? We have already seen many of them in St Justin's account. By St Gregory's time, the basic components of the Mass can be described as follows. In the first part of the Mass (known as the 'Mass of the Catechumens' because it could be attending by those still preparing for baptism), we have the scripture readings, culminating in the solemn proclamation of the Gospel, followed by a homily. Chants such as the Introit, Kyrie and Gloria were added gradually. After this came the 'Mass of the Faithful', attended only by the baptised. This again followed the most ancient models. There was the offering of bread, and of wine mixed with water. Then the Eucharistic Prayer containing the Words of Consecration and concluding with a Doxology - by the time of St Gregory this had already assumed the form of the Roman Canon, still used exclusively in the Extraordinary Form (and retained as Eucharistic Prayer I in the Ordinary Form). Gregory the Great himself placed the 'Our Father' directly after the Canon, and also by this time the Kiss of Peace had moved to its current position just before Communion. Communion itself was preceded by the Fraction, or Breaking of Bread, which was done with considerable solemnity, and after Communion Mass concluded with the Dismissal (*Ite, missa est*). Again, this part of the Mass was gradually adorned with suitable chants, such as the Offertory and Communion verses (which like the Introit were invariably taken from Scripture) and the *Agnus Dei*, introduced by Pope Sergius, c.700 AD. We must add to the above the three very important prayers known as the 'orations' - the Collect, Secret and Post-Communion prayers. These prayers of the celebrant, which again owe their composition to this period (5th-7th Century) reflect the particular characteristics of the Roman Rite, a spirit summed up by Dom Fernand Cabrol as 'simplicity, a certain austerity, and good sense'.[6] A more modern writer has this to say: 'In the orations we have the voice of the Roman Church, which adopted the heritage of the Roman Empire, transforming a universalism of Church and State into a spiritual universalism. Schooled by contact with the most brilliant examples of ancient rhetoric, the matter of the Church's prayer is here shaped most elegantly into priceless forms... The Roman Church never showed herself more beautiful than in these orations, which are a school of sacred sentiment. They express the distinctive nature of the Catholic Church, her concern for the sinner, her cautious guidance of souls, her dependence on the treasury of grace with which she has been endowed, her hope that hardened hearts will eventually be softened.'[7]

The Extraordinary Form of the Mass has preserved many of these beautiful priestly prayers. It has also preserved all those 'essential elements' of the Rite outlined above, inherited from the time of St Justin and codified by St Gregory. Little wonder it has sometimes been dubbed 'the Gregorian Rite'.

Charlemagne and the Middle Ages

Though the 'spirit' of the Roman Rite was fixed by the time of St Gregory, nevertheless the Mass continued to grow organically for many centuries. Gregory himself had great missionary zeal, and as the Roman Empire collapsed, so there were many new tribes to be converted to Christianity. It is interesting that although the Liturgy until this time had been celebrated in the vernacular (Aramaic, Greek, Latin etc) there never seems to have been a serious attempt to translate the Mass into the languages of these 'new peoples' of Europe. There were probably two reasons for this. Firstly, Latin, the language of Rome, could be seen as a unifying force on a divided continent. Secondly, it would have been very difficult to translate complex theological doctrines, worked out so laboriously at the Ecumenical Councils of the Church, into the languages and dialects of the newcomers. It has to be said that neither of these factors has diminished with time.

One person who appreciated the value of Latin, and the Roman Rite, as a unifying force was Charlemagne, who was crowned Emperor of the West by Pope Leo III on Christmas Day 800. Although no man of culture himself (he could barely write his name) Charlemagne gathered around him a brilliant court of scholars, including the Englishman, Alcuin of York. Under their influence, the Roman Rite was introduced all over Charlemagne's dominions, although embellished with additions from local 'Gallican' Rites. These tended to be rather more florid than the austere Roman prayers, but eventually the Romans came to accept them into their own Rite, and even welcome them as adornments. As well as more elaborate prayers, vestments, art, music and ceremonial all multiplied as well, and this process continued throughout the Middle Ages. Sometimes these new elements were a response to heresy - doubts cast on the reality of Transubstantiation inspired genuflection before the Blessed Sacrament, and the Elevation accompanied by torches and incense. Such inspiring and symbolic ceremonies also helped the illiterate and less educated to take part in the liturgy. Though it used to be commonplace to scoff at the piety of the Middle Ages, the work of Eamon Duffy[8] and other revisionist scholars has shown this to be untenable. Though they might not be able to understand every word being uttered in the sanctuary, even the simplest of the faithful could be moved to open their hearts to the rhythm of the liturgy, and participate at the deepest level in the Sacrifice being offered.

On the eve of the Reformation, the Roman Rite had spread its influence across the whole of Western Europe and into every area of life. Although different 'uses' of the Mass were celebrated from place to place - for example, the Sarum Use in England - these owed a great deal to the Roman Liturgy, and were often almost indistinguishable from it. Local customs flourished, yet the essential elements were never extinguished. A pilgrim could have travelled from Walsingham to Rome, from Paris to Santiago, attending Mass in every church, cathedral and chapel along the route, and yet in all of them he would have felt at home. Indeed, he would feel just as much at home if he attended a celebration of the Extraordinary Form today.

The Reformation and the Council of Trent

The Protestant Reformers - Luther, Calvin, Zwingli and so on - all rejected certain elements of the Catholic Faith. They likewise rejected the Catholic liturgy, in which the doctrines of that faith were expressed. Indeed, Protestantism might even be called an 'anti-liturgical heresy', in that the Protestant leaders had very little time for rites, ceremonies or prayers derived from the past. Turning their backs on the living Tradition, they devised their own, new services based on their own antiquarian researches, which frequently bore little or no resemblance to the authentic practices of the early Church. The worst aspect of this was that they downplayed the importance of the Eucharist, savagely attacking the doctrines of Sacrifice and Transubstantiation in the Mass, and, in most cases, celebrated the 'Lord's Supper' only infrequently.

The Church's response to the Protestant challenge was the Council of Trent, which met for a considerable period between 1545 and 1563. While determined to defend the Church against her enemies, the bishops assembled at Trent were by no means closed to genuine reform. They knew that corruption and scandal were present in the religious orders; that the lower clergy could be ignorant and unchaste, and the higher clergy avaricious and worldly. Moreover, they accepted that there were genuine abuses present in the liturgy itself. With so many local customs allowed to flourish, problems inevitably arose. Saints were celebrated who had never existed; ceremonies sometimes owed more to pagan tradition than to genuine Christianity, and services grew so complex and prolix that they did little to foster piety. The answer, the Bishops decided, was to impose the 'pure' Roman Rite upon the whole of the Western Church, and to do away with local uses. Henceforth, one Missal would be used by everyone. However, with the prudence and generosity typical of the Catholic Church, the bishops also decided that any Rite which could prove itself more than 200 years old should be permitted to continue.

This 'Tridentine' Missal was promulgated by Pope St Pius V in 1570. It is, in fact, virtually identical to the Missal approved for the City of Rome in 1474. As a recent scholar has written: 'The Tridentine liturgical reform, initiated in order to correct abuse and ensure doctrinal orthodoxy, was thoroughly traditional. It produced nothing radically new'.[9] The Fathers of Trent had succeeded in preserving the best from the past, while also equipping the Church for the future.

From Trent to Vatican II

In 1913, Fr Adrian Fortescue[10] wrote as follows:

'Our missal is still that of Pius V. We may be very thankful that his commission was so scrupulous to keep or restore the old Roman tradition. Essentially the Missal of Pius V is the Gregorian Sacramentary; that again is formed from the Gelasian Book, which depends upon the Leonine collection ... So our Mass goes back, without essential change, to the age when it first developed out of the oldest Liturgy of all. It is still redolent of that Litrurgy, of the days when Caesar ruled the world and thought he could stamp out the faith of Christ, when our fathers met together before dawn and sang a hymn to Christ as to a God ... there is not in Christendom another rite so ancient as ours.'

What Fortescue wrote is true. From the time of Trent onwards, there was never a wholesale reform of the Roman Rite until Vatican II. Of course, there were prayers added for newly canonised saints, and some new prefaces; certain Popes made other minor changes. Pius XII in 1955 made quite a radical change to the Holy Week services, removing many medieval elements. Nevertheless, the Missal itself remained virtually unchanged, and this was still the case in 1962, when Blessed John XXIII promulgated what is now recognised as the last typical edition of the Extraordinary Form of the Roman Rite.

Following Vatican II, a wholesale reform of the liturgy *did* take place, and the Extraordinary Form, we must say, virtually disappeared. It was kept alive only by a handful of dedicated groups - such as the Latin Mass Society in England and the international *Una Voce* movement worldwide. Yet as Pope Benedict has reminded us, this form of Mass 'was never juridically abrogated and consequently in principle was always permitted'. *Summorum Pontificum* has now created a juridical situation, and opens a new chapter in the history of the Mass. Access to the older liturgy is no longer the preserve of a privileged few - a whole new generation will be able to experience for itself these treasures preserved from the past.

An Outline of the Extraordinary Form

'It behoves us all to preserve the riches which have developed in the Church's faith and prayer, and to give them their proper place'

In the final part of our booklet we will give a brief outline of the structure of the Extraordinary Form. Some elements, of course, will be common to both Forms of the Roman Rite - some are now found only in the Extraordinary Form. We will begin by saying a few words about the different ways in which the Extraordinary Form can be offered. A Mass said simply by a priest with a server is known as a **Low Mass**. There are also two form of Solemn Mass, when there will be singing and more elaborate ceremonies. At a **High Mass**, the celebrant is assisted by a deacon and subdeacon - incense and lights are always used. A *Missa Cantata* (Sung Mass) is similar but without the assistance of deacon and subdeacon. The texts and basic structure of the Mass are the same however the Mass is offered.

The Introit

We begin with the verse called the *Introit*. Although at Low Mass it is read after the Prayers of Preparation, at

Solemn Mass it is sung as the priest approaches the altar, and this was the ancient practice. At the time of St Gregory the Great it was a song sung as the clergy processed into church. The text was taken from Scripture - especially the psalms - and was much longer than the vestige which remains today. The psalms in these ancient introits reflected the underlying 'theme' of the Mass, varying according to the season; thus joyful psalms were used in Eastertide, penitential ones in Lent. Even today, the introit sets the tone for everything else to follow. Note that in the Roman Rite the chants of the Mass (the Introit, Offertory and Communion) are almost always taken from Scripture itself.

The Prayers of Preparation

These prayers (often called the 'Prayers at the foot of the altar') begin with the Sign of the Cross, and include Psalm 42, with its antiphon 'I will go unto the altar of God'. This is followed by the *Confiteor* (I confess...) and the short prayers said quietly by the priest as he approaches and reverences the altar with a kiss. The second of these prayers (*Oramus te*) refers to the relics placed within the altar. The origin of these 'preparatory prayers' can be traced to around the 7th Century, although they varied considerably in content and form. In the Middle Ages they were often said quietly by the priest as he walked to the sanctuary. Psalm 42 is especially appropriate to this point in the Mass. In the early centuries it was sometimes sung by all the faithful at the Easter Vigil, a song of rebirth and reverence for God. These are the thoughts we should have in our minds as Mass begins.

The Kyrie

The *Kyrie* is almost the only part of the old Latin liturgy still recited in Greek. It has its origins in the long litanies which form part of the Greek liturgy. Etheria, a famous pilgrim to Jerusalem, heard such chants being sung there about 500 AD, and the practice had certainly reached Rome by the time of St Gregory. By the ninth century, it had been fixed that each petition (*Kyrie eleison, Christe eleison, Kyrie eleison*) should be sung three times, making nine in all, and the Extraordinary Form retains this custom. Some have seen in this a reference to the threefold nature of God (Father, Son and Holy Spirit) or to the nine choirs of angels. The *Kyrie* is a beautiful expression of our need of God and desire for his mercy, and forms part of every Mass.

The Gloria

The *Gloria* is used only on Sundays and feasts - because of its joyful character it is not used even on Sundays in penitential seasons such as Advent or Lent. The opening words are those the angels sang over Bethlehem at the birth of Christ (*Lk* 2:14) and the remainder of the hymn was composed in early Christian times following the pattern of the psalms. Like the *Kyrie*, it may have originated in the East. Some think it was introduced to the West by St Hilary of Poitiers (+366) and again it had certainly reached Rome by St Gregory's time. In the Middle Ages, when the *Gloria* was sung it was often 'troped', that is, certain phrases were added (such as praises of Our Lady, or even the name of the local king or ruler). This was one of the practices outlawed by St Pius V in 1570.

The Collect

We spoke at length about the Collect when discussing the history of the Mass. These prayers form one of the oldest, most characteristic and most beautiful parts of the Roman Rite. The name 'collect' perhaps refers to the fact that the celebrant at this point 'collects together' the prayers of the entire assembly (a fact symbolised by the extending and closing of his hands as he says '*oremus*'). It also reminds us that the prayers of the liturgy belong to all - they are the worship of the *plebs collecta*, the gathered people of God. The collects are always addressed to the Trinity in unity, and when the priest mentions the holy name of Jesus he bows his head. At some Masses there may be more than one collect - for example, when the feast of more than one saint falls on the same day.

The Epistle

As we saw in St Justin, readings from Scripture form one of the oldest parts of the Mass. In the older form of the liturgy, the first reading is known as the Epistle, because it is most often taken from one of the Apostolic Letters of the New Testament, but it can also be from the Old Testament, especially during Lent. On some penitential days - for example, the so-called 'ember days' - there may be many readings. At a High Mass, the Epistle is sung by the subdeacon. According to *Summorum Pontificum*, both the epistle and Gospel can be proclaimed directly in the vernacular, but it is also permitted to follow the traditional custom and read them in Latin. In Great Britain (and many other places) it has long been a custom to proclaim the readings in the vernacular *after* they have been read in Latin, particularly if there is to be a sermon.

Gradual, Alleluia, Tract, Sequence

These verses mark a moment of preparation between the Epistle and Gospel. At a Solemn Mass they are sung. The Gradual and Alleluia are used at most Masses. The Gradual was originally sung by a singer standing on a step (*gradus*). Like the Introit, it is a song taken from Scripture, most often the psalms. 'Alleluia' is a Jewish expression of joy (Praise the Lord!) used by Christians since the earliest times. It is especially appropriate to Eastertide, and the joy of the Resurrection, and for that reason is never used in Lent or in the short season which prepares for Lent (Septuagesima). At those times, it is substituted by the Tract, another chant taken from Scripture. Occasionally a long chant called a Sequence immediately precedes the Gospel. Unusually, these are not directly Scriptural, and are not Roman in origin, but introduced from other parts of Christendom during the Middle Ages. Before the Tridentine Reforms there were many sequences in use, but St Pius V retained only 5. These are the *Victimae Paschali Laudes*, for Easter and its Octave, *Lauda Sion* (said to have been composed by St Thomas Aquinas) at Corpus Christi, *Veni Sancte Spiritus* at Pentecost, the *Dies Irae* for Requiems and the *Stabat Mater* used to commemorate the sorrows of Our Lady.

The Gospel

The Gospel is proclaimed at the 'North' side of the sanctuary, whereas the Epistle was read at the 'South' side. At Low Mass the server moves the Missal from one side to the other, while the priest recites the *munda cor*, a prayer of preparation and purification. At High Mass the deacon sings the Gospel facing North, while the subdeacon holds the book for him. The Gospel Book is treated with great reverence - it is kissed by the priest and accompanied by lights and incense at Solemn Mass. All present make the Sign of the Cross on their forehead, lips and breast when the reading is announced. These things remind us that the lessons are not meant only for our instruction - they are also a genuine 'epiphany', a manifestation of God.

The Homily and Creed

The current law of the Church requires that a homily, or sermon, be given on every Sunday and Holiday of Obligation. The homily is not considered an integral part of the Extraordinary Form, and you will notice that the celebrant usually removes his maniple (sometimes his chasuble as well) before beginning to preach. In the Eastern Church, the homily is usually given at the end of Mass, after the liturgy as such is concluded. The Creed is only recited in the Extraordinary Form on Sundays and very important feasts. Originally part of the baptismal liturgy, this profession of faith crept into the Mass as a testimony and encouragement to orthodoxy. 'Let the Creed resound' ordered the Council of Toledo 'so that the true faith may be declared'. It is said that Rome was the last place to introduce the Creed into the Mass, on the grounds that the Church there had always kept the faith, and had no need to be reminded of what it consisted!

The Offertory

We saw the offering of bread, wine and water in St Justin. It is a necessary part of the Mass. The action is accompanied by the Offertory verse, again one of those Scriptural chants intended to be sung. Then come six prayers said quietly by the priest, all medieval in origin and very beautiful. The first, *Suscipe, sancte Pater*, is used at the offering of the bread. It contains the phrase *hanc immaculatam hostiam* ('this immaculate victim'), which some see as inappropriate at this point of the Mass. However, as Adrian Fortescue points out: 'It is an anticipation of the consecration, a dramatic misplacement of which all liturgies have examples'. After this, the wine is poured into the chalice, and the water blessed before being added. In the Middle Ages this mixture of the water with the wine (originating, in all probability, at the Last Supper itself) was seen as symbolising the union of human nature with the divinity made possible by the Incarnation, and this is alluded to in the prayer of blessing. Having offered the wine, the priest bows and says a prayer of supplication (*In spiritu humilitatis*) before invoking the Holy Spirit over the elements to be consecrated (*Veni, sanctificator*). He then washes his hands, for St Thomas Aquinas says 'it seems indecent that we should approach so great a sacrament with hands soiled'. This action is accompanied by the words of

Psalm 25: *Lavabo inter innocentes* - this is not one of the ancient chants of the Mass but rather a private devotion of the priest. The last of the Offertory prayers is also the longest - *Suscipe sancta Trinitas* - which again refers to the relics contained in the altar.

The Secret

Having said the *Suscipe*, the celebrant turns to the people for the *Orate fratres*, inviting them to join their own spiritual sacrifices to the Sacrifice of Christ which he is about to offer at the altar. This is a medieval prayer. He then reads the Secret, which is an 'oration' similar to the Collect. It is called secret because originally it was always read in a low voice while the Offertory chant was being sung.

The Preface and Sanctus

The Preface can be seen as the beginning of the Canon, or Eucharistic Prayer. It is always a hymn of thanksgiving, appropriately since the word 'Eucharist' itself means 'thanksgiving'. However, it is distinct from the rest of the Canon insofar as it is variable. In the early Roman liturgy it seems there were a great many Prefaces - these had been reduced by the time of St Gregory, then expanded again in the Middle Ages and shrank back with Trent. The *Missale Romanum* of 1962 contains a comparatively small number of Prefaces. *Summorum Pontificum* suggests that 'some of the new Prefaces [of the Ordinary

Form] can and should be inserted into the old Missal'. Obviously this may only be done by authority of the Holy See, and never as a private initiative.

The Preface always ends with a reference to the angels, and continues naturally into the Sanctus. This text is based on Isaiah 6:3, and is extremely ancient. It is mentioned by Clement of Rome (+99) and Tertullian (+222). Of its very nature it lends itself to be sung, as it is at a Solemn Mass. Since many musical settings of the Mass are rather elaborate, it is now common to sing the second part of the Sanctus (*Benedictus qui venit...*) after the Consecration.

The Canon of the Mass

'Canon' means 'rule', because this part of the Mass is fixed or unchanging. It has been so for many centuries - essentially since the time of St Gregory. The Roman Canon is in fact one of the most ancient, characteristic and beautiful prayers of the whole Latin liturgy. Whole books could be written about it, but here space prevents us from doing it justice. We will just note one aspect which would probably strike someone attending the Extraordinary Form as a newcomer: the Canon is said inaudibly, the priest speaking so softly as to be barely able to hear his own voice. The historical origins of this are disputed, but it can add to the numinous and reverential atmosphere of this most holy part of the Mass.

Even at High Mass, with an elaborate musical setting, we know that every human voice will be hushed between the *Hanc igitur* and the elevation of the chalice. In our busy world, these few seconds of sacred silence are certainly something to be treasured.

The Lord's Prayer

We have already said that this was placed in its current position by St Gregory. The petition 'Give us this day our daily bread' makes it an appropriate preparation for Holy Communion. Note that in the Extraordinary Form (following the old Roman custom) the *Pater noster* is recited by the priest alone, except for the last clause, '*sed libera nos a malo*'.

The Fraction

This action goes right back to the Last Supper (the Jewish people always broke, rather than cut their bread). In the New Testament the whole Mass was known as 'the breaking of bread' (*Ac* 2:42). Although hardly noticed today, it is an important moment, full of meaning. We remember, for example, that it was in 'the breaking of bread' that the disciples recognised the Risen Lord at Emmaus (*Lk* 24:13 - 35). Again, the little particle of the Host which is dropped into the chalice is a mystical symbol of the Resurrection, the reunion of Jesus' Body and Blood which were separated by his death on the Cross.

Agnus Dei and Rite of 'Pax'

Introduced to the Roman Rite from the East c700, the words of the Agnus Dei probably formed part of a longer litany once sung at this point. In the Requiem Mass the words are slightly changed. '*Miserere nobis*' becomes '*dona eis requiem*', and '*dona nobis pacem*' becomes '*dona eis requiem sempiternam*'. The mention of 'peace' introduces the rite of the 'Pax', or Kiss of Peace, performed only at High Mass (and never at Requiems). This is not merely a general peace shared among friends, but is seen to begin specifically in the Sacrifice on the altar, and then to flow out upon the Church.

Holy Communion

Holy Communion completes the Sacrifice of the Mass, and it is necessary and indispensable that the celebrating priest communicates. The faithful may receive Communion provided that they fulfil the usual conditions, i.e. that they are in a state of grace and have observed the Eucharistic fast.

The priest communicates first, the people after him. Showing them the Host, the priest again refers to Jesus as the Paschal Lamb: '*Ecce Agnus Dei…*', 'Behold the Lamb of God…' The response comes in the words of the centurion at Carphanum: '*Domine non sum dignus…*', 'Lord I am not worthy…'

You will notice in the Extraordinary Form that Communion is received kneeling, on the tongue and under one form (in the species of bread). We kneel because this is the generally accepted form of reverence in the West. In the early Church the congregation stood throughout the Mass, but once kneeling was introduced at certain moments out of reverence, it was obviously appropriate that people should kneel to receive the Blessed Sacrament as well.[11] Similarly, the Sacred Host is placed directly upon the tongue out of reverence, and to prevent the danger of Hosts being stolen or profaned - this became a factor as soon as the non-baptised were admitted to what had originally been 'the Mass of the Faithful'. Lastly, Communion under the form of bread alone also developed for reasons of reverence (to prevent any danger of the Precious Blood being spilt) and also to reinforce the theological truth that 'since Christ is sacramentally present under each of the species, Communion under the species of bread alone makes it possible to receive all the fruit of Eucharistic grace' (*Catechism of the Catholic Church*, #1390).

The Communion verse and Postcommunion

The Communion verse is another example of those scriptural chants like the Introit and Offertory verse. Similarly, the Postcommunion follows the pattern of the Collect and the Secret. During Lent there is an additional prayer called the *oratio super populum*, a prayer over the people suitable to this particular liturgical season (these Lenten prayers have been restored to the Ordinary Form in the most recent edition of the *Missale Romanum*, published in 2002 and currently awaiting translation).

The Dismissal and Blessing

Anciently, the Mass ended with the words of the dismissal (sung by the deacon at High Mass) '*Ite, missa est*' - it is from this phrase that we get our word 'Mass'. The phrase may also remind us that we are a missionary people, and we are sent out from the Mass to be apostles to the world around us. The blessing follows the dismissal because it is a later development. Before giving the blessing the priest bows and says the prayer Placeat placed here by St Pius V: 'Grant that the Sacrifice which I, unworthy as I am, have offered in the presence of your majesty may be acceptable...'

The Last Gospel

This is the beginning of St John's Gospel (*Jn* 1:1-14), which has fascinated Christians since the earliest times. Rather like the Prayers at the foot of the Altar, the last Gospel was originally said as a private thanksgiving by the priest as he returned to the sacristy (this is still done by the Bishop when he has celebrated a Pontifical Mass). All genuflect with the priest at the phrase '*Et Verbum caro factum est'*: 'And the Word was made flesh'. These are the words which celebrate the Incarnation - the coming of God among us, which is perpetuated and made real in the Mass.

Conclusion

In this short work we have tried to help the reader understand the important motives which led Pope Benedict to issue *Summorum Pontificum*, and have offered a very brief introduction to the ancient liturgy to which that document refers. In giving us this Motu Proprio the Holy Father has acted gently and courteously, imposing nothing on anyone, but issuing an invitation in which all the faithful are included. As a final word, therefore, let it be remembered that liturgy is not something which can live merely in the pages of books, but rather cries out to be celebrated. Those who have found this booklet helpful are now invited to go and seek out the *usus antiquior* for themselves.

Some suggestions for further reading

There are many books available on the traditional liturgy of the Church (and many more have been published since the appearance of *Summorum Pontificum*). These are just a selection which may be helpful.

Cardinal Joseph Ratzinger (Pope Benedict XVI), *The Spirit of the Liturgy*, Ignatius Press, San Francisco, 2000

Dom Fernand Cabrol, *On the Excellence of the Roman Liturgy* (reprinted), Farnborough Abbey Books, Farnborough, 2007

Fr Adrian Fortescue, *The Mass: A Study of the Roman Liturgy*, Longmans, London, 1912

Mgr Klaus Gamber, *The Reform of the Roman Liturgy*, Una Voce Press, California, 1993

Dr Laurence Hemming, *Worship as a Revelation: The past, present and future of Catholic Liturgy*, Burns and Oates, London, 2008

Uwe Michael Lang, Turning towards the Lord: Orientation in liturgical prayer, Ignatius Press, San Francisco, 2004

Martin Mosebach, *The heresy of formlessness*, Ignatius Press, San Francisco, 2006

Aidan Nichols OP, *Looking at the Liturgy*, Ignatius Press, San Francisco, 1996

Dr Alcuin Reid, *The organic development of the Liturgy*, Farnborough Abbey Books, Farnborough, 2004

Dr Alcuin Reid (editor), *Looking again at the question of the Liturgy with Cardinal Ratzinger (Proceedings of the Fontgombault Liturgical Conference)*, Farnborough Abbey Books, Farnborough, 2003.

Endnotes

1 Press conference in London, 14th June 2008.

2 Cardinal Joseph Ratzinger (Pope Benedict XVI), *Milestones: Memoirs 1927-1977*, Ignatius Press, San Francisco, 1998.

3 For an excellent summary of these conclusions see Uwe Michael Lang, *Turning towards the Lord*, Ignatius Press, San Francisco 2004

4 Pope Benedict XVI referred to the significance of this phrase in his General Audience, 23rd January 2008.

5 Again, Pope Benedict celebrated a public Mass '*ad orientem*' in the Sistine Chapel on the Solemnity of the Baptism of the Lord, 13th January 2008.

6 Dom Fernand Cabrol, *On the excellence of the Roman liturgy*, Farnborough Abbey Press, 2007, p6.

7 Martin Mosebach, *The Heresy of Formlessness*, Ignatius Press, 2006, p117.

8 Most importantly, *The Stripping of the Altars*, Yale University Press, 1994.

9 Alcuin Reid, *The Organic Development of the Liturgy*, Farnborough Abbey Press 2004, p35.

10 Fr Adrian Fortescue was a priest of the Archdiocese of Westminster, and a well-known liturgical authority of the early Twentieth Century. This quote is taken from his classic work, *The Mass: A Study of the Roman Liturgy*, 1912.

11 Since the Feast of Corpus Christi 2008, Pope Benedict XVI has returned to the tradition of giving Communion to kneeling communicants when he celebrates Papal Masses.

A world of Catholic reading
at your fingertips ...

CTS

... now online
Browse 500 titles at

www.cts-online.org.uk

Catholic Faith, Life, and Truth for all